SpringerBriefs in Finance

SpringerBriefs present concise summaries of cutting-edge research and practical applications across a wide spectrum of fields. Featuring compact volumes of 50 to 125 pages, the series covers a range of content from professional to academic. Typical topics might include: a timely report of state-of-the art analytical techniques, a bridge between new research results, as published in journal articles, and a contextual literature review, a snapshot of a hot or emerging topic, an in-depth case study or clinical example, and a presentation of core concepts that students must understand in order to make independent contributions. SpringerBriefs in Finance showcase emerging theory, empirical research, and practical application in corporate finance, banking, financial management, behavioral finance, financial markets, social and entrepreneurial finance, microfinance, and related fields, from a global author community. Briefs are characterized by fast, global electronic dissemination, standard publishing contracts, standardized manuscript preparation and formatting guidelines, and expedited production schedules.

Ralf Hohmann

Securities Lending and Repos

Instruments and Strategies for Excess Return

Springer

Ralf Hohmann
Hamburg, Germany

ISSN 2193-1720 ISSN 2193-1739 (electronic)
SpringerBriefs in Finance
ISBN 978-3-658-41983-7 ISBN 978-3-658-41984-4 (eBook)
https://doi.org/10.1007/978-3-658-41984-4

This Springer imprint is published by the registered company Springer Fachmedien Wiesbaden GmbH, part of Springer Nature.
The registered company address is: Abraham-Lincoln-Str. 46, 65189 Wiesbaden, Germany

About This Book

Securities lending and repos have different manifestations. Nevertheless, they are equivalent instruments with which market participants can realise an excess return. With selected transactions and selected strategies, returns can be achieved that are above the risk-free interest rate for corresponding maturities. To achieve this, market participants use differential arbitrage and compensatory arbitrage with different interest rates and premiums on the market. This is not pure short selling. The necessary procedure is described in this book and the corresponding formulas are derived. These transactions should change interest rates and premiums in the market, which then theoretically strive towards equilibrium. In this way, the market participants promote the efficiency of the market, and the resulting changes in costs and returns benefit all market participants.

Contents

FN.	Footnote
FT	Financial Times
HB	Handelsblatt
Hrsg.	editor
ibid.	Ibidem
if	applicable if necessary
i.e.	that is
IHT	International Herald Tribune
INYT	International New York Times
ISA	Insurance Supervision Act
KAGG	Capital Investment Act
KWG	German Banking Act
Mill.	Mill.
Mio	Million
Nr.	Number
No.	Number
o.O.	Without city/country/land
o.V.	Without author
or	respectively
p.	Page
possibly	Under certain circumstances
REPO	Repurchase Agreements
SEC	Securities And Exchange Commission
US	United States
USD	US Dollar
Vol	Volume
WPL	Securities Lending
Yr.	Year

List of Symbols

Aus	Compensation payment in T
C	Rate/price of a European call/call option
Er_t	Interest and investment income in T
F_t	Price of a future in t
$G_{Hed,E,T}$	Result of a hedge with borrowing in T
$G_{WPL,E,T}$	Profit Securities lending for borrowers in T
$G_{WPL,V,T}$	Profit Securities lending for lenders in T
K	Strike price of an option
K_t	Strike price of an option in t
§	Paragraph
%	Percent
Repo	Repo
r	Interest rate

List of Abbreviations

AG	Public limited company/Aktiengesellschaft
AIG	American International Group
AO	Tax code/Abgabenordnung
as a rule	as a rule
BAK	Federal Banking Supervisory Office
BBankG	Act on the Deutsche Bundesbank
BGB	Civil Code
Billion	Billion
BNP	Banque National de Paris
CAPM	Capital Asset Pricing Model
cf.	compare
DAX	German Share Index
CEDEL	Centrale de Livraison de Valeurs
CFD	Contracts for Difference
DB	Die Bank
DKV	German Kassenverein
DTB	German Futures Exchange
Ed.	Publisher
EDP	electronic data processing
EMT	Efficient Market Theory
ETFs	Exchange Traded Funds or Futures
EU	European Union
EUR	Euro
EUREX	European Exchange
e.g.	for example
esp. in	particular
e.V.	registered association
FAZ	Frankfurter Allgemeine Zeitung
ff.	furthermore following

About the Author

Ralf Hohmann studied business administration at the University of Hamburg. After his doctorate, he went to Frankfurt as a consultant for financial management. He then returned to Hamburg where he lives with his family and works as a managing director in several family businesses.

r_f	Risk-free interest rate
r_{REPO}	Repo rate in per cent
r_{WPL}	Lending fee/premium in percent
P	Rate/price of a put/put option
S	Price of the security/share
S_T	Price of the security/share in T
S_t	Price of the security/share in t
$S_{t,Repo}$	Price of a share sold via a repo
$S_{t,WPL}$	Price of a security lent via a securities lending transaction
t	Start of the time horizon
T	End of the time horizon
$(T - t)$	Period from T minus t
V	Assets/Cash
V_t	Value/price of the assets in t
$V_{t,REPO}$	Value/price of assets sold via a repo
WP	Security
WPL	Securities Lending

List of Figures

Chapter 1
Prologue

The historic price losses in 2008 and 2009 on the international securities markets followed the sub-prime crisis on the American mortgage markets. Bank insolvencies led to government holdings in individual banks Similarly, the central banks drastically cut interest rates as a supposed last-ditch rescue attempt to prevent the financial crisis from spreading. The extent of the price losses and subsequent gains led to historically high volatilities. Uncertainty with a view to the future and existential fears shaped the discussion of the events.

The crisis gave rise to new perspectives and assessments of stock exchange and over-the-counter investment decisions. In addition to attempts to explain what had happened, demands were made as to how money and capital markets should be regulated in the future. With the aim of avoiding a repetition of the events in the future through selected means, especially higher capital requirements were imposed on the banks involved. Likewise, many over-the-counter derivates were publicly outlawed as major triggers of the crisis. Securities lending was also temporarily banned in order to supposedly ease the pressure on share prices through a lack of short sales.

The opposite happened. Market participants were unable to hedge their cash market positions and suitable instruments were no longer available on the futures market. In order to reduce the risk, the only solution was to sell the positions without having to buy them back later. The corresponding selling pressure due to the uniform behaviour of many market participants increased, price losses widened.

Securities lending as a way of short selling is not only suitable for hedging cash market positions. Securities lending is also an essential prerequisite for valuing options on the futures market. Their valuation according to the option price theory is theoretically not possible without securities lending. If, at the same time, no derivatives are traded on the market as a substitute, the valuation of a portfolio of cash and futures market positions is difficult to practise. This is unacceptable for the annual financial statements of banks, insurance companies and other capital collection agencies.

R. Hohmann, *Securities Lending and Repos*, SpringerBriefs in Finance,
https://doi.org/10.1007/978-3-658-41984-4_1

The evaluation of regulatory and or political restrictions on securities lending and repos will be the subject of later investigations. This will be all the more the case if securities lending and repos are again the same or larger in volume than before the crisis.

The aim of this paper is to present different manifestations and specific transactions with securities lending and repos. With securities lending and repos, as well as with selected strategies, returns can be achieved that are above the risk-free interest rate for corresponding maturities. Market participants use differential arbitrage and compensatory arbitrage with different interest rates and premiums on the market to achieve an excess return. This is not pure short selling. Interest rates and premiums in the market should theoretically strive towards equilibrium through these transactions. In this way, market participants promote the efficiency of the market, and the resulting changes in premiums and interest rates benefit all market participants.

Chapter 2
Introduction and Course of the Study

Securities lending and repos are essential instruments for German cash and derivatives markets. They support trading on the cash markets and make transactions on the futures markets possible in the first place (Blitz and Illhardt 1990, p. 142). They improve the liquidity of the cash markets and increase the number of securities traded. Securities lending shortens the holding period of individual securities, if necessary, and the issue market finds support. Securities lending and repos increase market depth and facilitate the settlement of transactions on cash and futures markets (Limmert 1994, pp. 78–79; Faulkner 2005, p. 3). At the same time, they make it possible to generate additional income from existing positions through hedging and arbitrage opportunities. For the valuation of options and futures, securities lending is outstanding (Jurgeit 1989, pp. 102–108; Hohmann 1996, pp. 33–39). Securities lending and repos increase market efficiency, the efficient market line rises.

On international spot and futures markets, securities lending and repos are among the most frequently used instruments (Faulkner 2005, p. 63). Securities lending had a daily volume of USD 1.7 trillion worldwide in 2012 (o.V. 4.9.2013b, p. 2). Repos had an outstanding volume of 185.6 billion euros in Germany on 13.6.2013 (o.V. 24.9.2013a, p. 3). These figures are impressive in comparison to the transactions on German futures markets in 2010 with 1.9 billion contracts (o.V. 24.9.2013a, p. 3).

Part 2 of this paper presents the manifestations of securities lending and repo transactions. Legal basics and transactions with securities lending and repos are shown. This is followed by the different market participants and their motives for entering into the respective positions. Particularly examined are the proceeds and costs as well as the risks and collateral that can result from individual positions. This is followed by a discussion of assumptions for German spot and futures markets The necessary assumptions are compared with the reality on German financial markets and their realism is discussed.

Part 3 shows different strategies that can be set up with securities lending and/or repos. Strategies with securities lending and futures contracts on shares and share

R. Hohmann, *Securities Lending and Repos*, SpringerBriefs in Finance,
https://doi.org/10.1007/978-3-658-41984-4_2

indices are examined. A comparable procedure follows for strategies with securities lending and options. The identical procedure for repos follows. This is followed by strategies that combine securities lending and repos. Here again strategies with securities lending, repos, stocks and the respective indices and options are to be examined. For reasons of space, bonds, bond indices and corresponding derivatives are not presented in this text.

The paper concludes with a summary and an outlook on future topics of investigation.

Chapter 3
Forms of Securities Lending and Repos

3.1 Securities Lending

3.1.1 Definition, Basic Forms and Special Forms

The legal basis for selected market participants is only briefly described below.

Securities lending is not a loan contract according to § 598 BGB. The lender transfers securities to a borrower for a certain period of time. It is therefore a loan in kind against payment within the meaning of §§ 607 ff. BGB, in which the borrower undertakes to return securities of the same kind and number (see Häuselmann and Wiesenbart 1990, p. 2129, Leez 2007, pp. 1–2) to the lender after the expiry of an agreed period. The borrower pays a borrowing fee to the lender as consideration at the end of the loan period. During the lending period, he must provide collateral equivalent to the value of the securities borrowed plus a margin of safety (Sloan 1997, p. 247).

Securities lending does not correspond to a loan according to § 19 KWG. §§ 13–18 KWG are also not applicable. Principles I and Ia of the BAK apply to banks whose lending transactions are risk-bearing transactions and must therefore be backed by equity capital. In the case of securities lending transactions, however, there is an obligation to notify the Bundesbank in accordance with §24 of the German Banking Act (KWG). If banks lend securities, these are not considered deposits or money borrowed, as they represent material delivery obligations pursuant to §16 of the Federal Banking Act. They are not subject to the minimum reserve requirement. Cash collateral transferred to the lender, on the other hand, is subject to minimum reserve requirements (Limmert 1994, p. 7).

The investment regulations of the Insurance Supervision Act apply to securities lending transactions by insurance companies. § 54 of the Insurance Supervision Act regulates how high the percentage of free investment of the cover pool and the other tied assets can be. The 5% limit may be exceeded under certain circumstances.

R. Hohmann, *Securities Lending and Repos*, SpringerBriefs in Finance,
https://doi.org/10.1007/978-3-658-41984-4_3

Sections 8 and 9 KAGG regulate the investment principles for investment funds as capital investment companies. As special assets of capital investment companies, securities lending is not permitted (Limmert 1994, pp. 7–8).

Hedge funds and private equity market participants are not yet subject to any special legal restrictions. From 2009 onwards, however, it seemed as if the legislator wanted to include these market participants and their transactions in securities lending and repos in the regulatory framework.

The legal basis cannot be presented further here. The aim of this paper is to present strategies with securities lending and repo and their feasibility. The question of legal admissibility for individual market participants is the task of more in-depth legal work.

Market participants with first-class credit ratings can or could borrow securities on selected markets without having to provide collateral. Likewise, it is or was possible to sell securities that were not previously borrowed. This circumstance is a prerequisite for uncovered securities lending (see Kumar 2015, pp. 120–121).

The property and management rights during securities lending can only be briefly described (see Limmert 1994, pp. 19–22, Cahn and Ostler 2008, pp. 23–24). At the beginning of securities lending, the lender transfers the securities to the borrower's securities account for a certain period of time. The borrower thus becomes the beneficial owner of the securities and has the possibility to dispose of these securities accordingly. The lender, however, continues to be the owner in the sense of § 598 BGB, despite the loss of the power of disposal over the securities.

The lender remains the owner of the lent securities, he is thus the beneficiary of the property and management rights to which the securities are entitled. Asset items such as interest and dividends, subscription rights or bonus shares, exchange offers or tax credits go to the lender. If these positions do not exist in direct form, e.g. through compensation payments, the borrower passes them on to the lender. Voting rights of shares, however, remain with the owner, the borrower, on the day of the general meeting, unless otherwise provided for in individual contracts (Ledwig 2017, pp. 6–7, 8–11; Jörg 2020, pp. 25–26).

The borrowed securities are to be attributed to the borrower according to § 39 AO, accounting at the lender is not possible. Interest income from securities, e.g. from interest-bearing securities or cash deposits invested on the money market, also accrue to the borrower (see Oegerli 1991, p. 43, Jacklin and Felsenthal 1997, p. 116).

The attribution of ownership, possession and income between lender and borrower are shown in Fig. 3.1.

The lender's profit consists of the lending fee for the securities lending plus the settlement payments minus the interest and capital gains from collateral provided or received and provisions for any intermediaries (Jensen and Scheetz 1997, pp. 90–94; Chichilinsky 2012, pp. 5–8; Parnes 2020, pp. 3–4, 37–43).

The profit of securities lending for the lender in T can be represented by formula 1.

Fig. 3.1 Attribution of ownership, possession and income

Attribution of:	Lender	Borrower
Property	x	
Possession		x
Income from lending security	x	
Income from collateral security	(x)	x
Voting rights		(x)

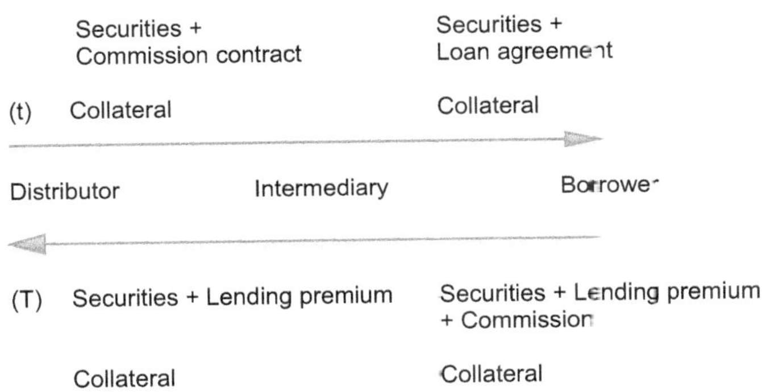

Fig. 3.2 Agent method

$$\text{Formula 1:} G_{WPL,V,T} = (S_t * r_{WPL})^{(T\text{-}t)} + Aus\text{-}E_{rt}$$

with: $G_{WPL,\ V,\ T}$ = Profit securities lending for lender in T
S_t = Price of the security in t
Aus = Compensation payments in T
E_{rt} = Interest and investment income in T
r_{WPL} = Lending fee or premium in percentages
t = beginning of the time horizon
T = End of the time horizon

The form or characteristics of securities lending transactions in Germany are not legally prescribed (Limmert 1994, p. 10; Kokologiannis 2012, p. 38). There are different methods of individual transactions, as shown below.

In the agent method, an intermediary steps between the lender and the borrower. Often a bank acts as an intermediary or broker. It concludes a securities lending transaction with the borrower in the bank's own name, but for the account of the customer. As a commission agent, the bank takes over the brokerage of the transaction as well as the formal tasks of executing the transaction and receives a commission for this (Limmert 1994, p. 8; Nazzaro 2005, pp. 67–72). For existing credit risks, it demands collateral for the assumption of these risks.

Figure 3.2 shows the approach of market participants in the agent method (see Cohen et al. 2004, p. 11).

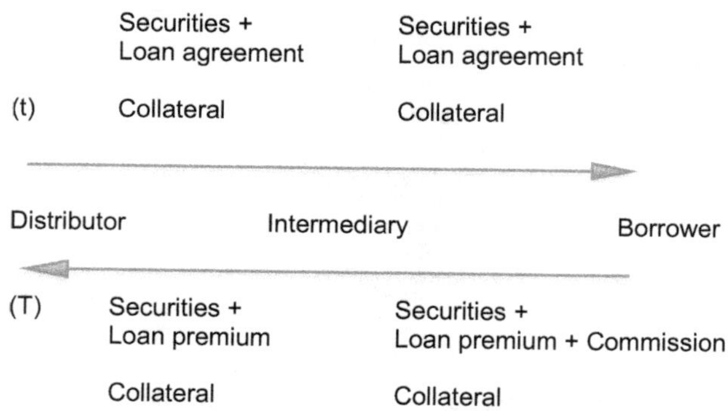

Fig. 3.3 Principal method

The procedure and presentation of the agent method are similar to those of interest rate swaps. In interest rate swaps, short and long-term interest payment obligations are exchanged between two market participants. Often a bank acts as an intermediary, bringing the two swap partners together (see Van Horne 1994, pp. 193–205).

In the principal method, however, the lender and the intermediary act di-rectly with each other. The intermediary acts as a borrower who uses the borrowed securities for himself or lends them on to third market participants (Faulkner and Sackville 1997, pp. 54–55; Nazzaro 1997, pp. 72–73).

Figure 3.3 shows the procedure of the market participants in the principal method (see Limmert 1994, p. 9).

Like the agent method, the principal method has parallels to interest rate swaps with an intermediary.

3.1.2 *Market Participants and Motives*

Lenders and borrowers are always involved in securities lending, possibly also intermediaries. The motives of the market participants, their proceeds and costs as well as risks and collateral required and provided for their transactions are shown below.

3.1.2.1 Lender

The lender of securities is the owner and holder of the securities. He transfers them to the borrower. At the same time, he underwrites to take back these securities from the borrower after a certain period of time. The lender receives a lending premium from the borrower for the lending. The premium varies in amount. It amounts to 0.1–2.5% of the value of the loaned stocks in t and 1–1.75% of the value of the loaned interest-bearing securities in t. The lender earns income from the loaned securities. The lender earns income from the securities, even without changes in the price of the securities lent (Kirchner 2007, p. 76; Landgraf 2003, p. 231). To this must be added any interest payments and dividends.

The amount of the premium differs between individual market participants due to different credit ratings, individual strategies or special time horizons. It also varies on individual trading platforms, such as the lending system of the banks or the Deutsche Kassenverein.

One motive for securities lending for the lender is the reduction of management fees for the securities portfolio. Loaned securities are no longer in the portfolio during the loan period and custody fees are waived for this time.

The lender can also generate income from collateral received. If he receives cash collateral, he can invest it at interest on the money market for the duration of the securities lending. The interest income thus increases the simple contractual premium from the lending transaction. The situation is different if the lender has to transfer the interest income back to the borrower at the end of the loan. The lender should then earn interest income that is higher than the interest demanded by the borrower.

Another motive for the lender is the short-term creation of liquidity if the lender does not want to sell any positions. He receives the agreed lending premium at the end of the securities lending and can also invest the cash collateral received individually during the term.

For foreign market participants, the strategy of dividend stripping is important. In this case, market participants can achieve corporate tax credits through securities lending if the period of the loan exceeds the dividend payment date (see Godek 2001, pp. B11–B12).

3.1.2.2 Borrower

The borrower receives securities of which he does not become the owner, but which come into his possession. The borrower undertakes to return these securities to the lender in due time. The borrower pays the lender the lending premium as a fee for the loan.

The motives of the borrower vary. Mostly, the borrower uses the securities lending to carry out short sales. To do this, he sells the borrowed securities in order to buy them back later at a lower, more favourable price. The positive amount from the sale in t minus the purchase of the same securities in T, minus the premium to be paid for the period (T − t), is the result of the short sale. The result of the short sale is shown in formula 2.

$$\text{Formula 2 : Result of a short sale for the borrower in T :}$$
$$G_{WPL,E,T} = S_t - S_T - S_t{}^{*}\, r_{WPL}{}^{(T-t)}$$

If a positive result of the short sale is the sole objective of the market participant, then the motive of this securities lending is speculation. There is then no simultaneous long position in shares.

If the market participant has securities in his portfolio, then hedging against falling prices is another motive of the short seller. If a negative result of the securities lending is acceptable to him, if the lent securities possibly rise in price, then he can secure an existing position in securities against losses. As before in speculation, the market participant hopes to be able to buy back the securities sold in t at a reduced price in T. The desired positive outcome of the lending transaction is a loss. The desired positive result of the short sale will then compensate for the losses of a long position in the same securities. The lending fee/premium to be paid is then the price of the hedge. The result of the hedge in T for the entire position $G_{Hed,\,E,\,T}$ is shown in formula 3.

$$\text{Formula 3 : Hedge with short sale :}$$
$$G_{Hed,E,T} = S_T - S_t + S_t - S_T - S_t{}^{*}\, r_{WPL}{}^{(T-t)} = S_t{}^{*}\, r_{wpl}{}^{(T-t)}$$

Arbitrage is another motive for the borrower to use securities lending. Prices on the futures markets for options and futures usually follow the option price theory or the arbitrage theory with financial futures. If the prices deviate from their theoretically determined prices, then there should be an opportunity for arbitrage. To do this, the market participant buys the undervalued position and simultaneously sells the overvalued position (see Heinke 1992, pp. B23–B24). If he does not hold the position to be sold, he borrows it through securities lending. With regard to the option price theory and the arbitrage approach with financial futures, it becomes clear that securities lending has a prominent significance for futures markets (see Cox and Rubinstein 1985, Faulkner 2000, p. 4).

Achieving opportunity proceeds can also be a motive for the borrower. In the case of a sale of securities held in the portfolio, the market participant uses borrowed securities to meet the delivery obligation more quickly and to undercut the delivery date. This results in a faster payment of the sales proceeds to the seller's account (Landgraf 1991, p. 41).

Securities lending can also serve as an alternative form of investing financial resources in the money market. The borrower provides cash as collateral, which the lender must invest profitably, usually in the money market or in his own portfolio. The return on the collateral provided then generally accrues to the borrower.

Tax reasons are also relevant for short sales, e.g. when securities are sold but the taxes from the sale are to be avoided. The economically same transaction can be realised with securities lending if a position in securities is to be shown in the balance sheet on a reporting date, but not increases in value accrued in the meantime (see Oho and v. Hülst 1992, pp. 2584–2586).

3.1.2.3 Intermediaries

Intermediaries bring lenders and borrowers together when they cannot carry out lending transactions directly. Intermediaries then usually assume part of the risk and provide liquidity. For this they demand a financial fee.

In the agent method, the bank receives a commission for arranging the securities lending between the lender and the borrower.

In the principal method, the bank acts as a contract partner between the lender and the borrower. The motive here is for the bank as intermediary to have a share in the payment flows and to receive a part of the premium. It is also conceivable that the intermediary receives a share of the interest on the borrower's collateral (see Pantel 2000, pp. 21–22).

The different motives of the individual market participants can be illustrated in Fig. 3.4.

3.1.3 Proceeds and Costs, Risks and Collateral

The proceeds from positions in securities lending transactions result from the contractual provisions of the respective transaction. The same applies to the associated costs. Each securities lending transaction also involves risks for which collateral must be provided. These points are examined below for the respective market participants.

Fig. 3.4 Different motives of market participants

Motifs	Lender	Borrower	Intermediary
Reduction of administrative costs	X		
Realising proceeds from collateral received or provided	(X)	X	(X)
Short-term liquidity provision	X		
Dividend stripping	(X)		
Receipt of premiums	X		X
Speculation in risk position/ hedge		X	
Arbitrage		X	
Achieving opportunity revenue through faster crediting		X	

3.1.3.1 Lender

The lender receives a premium from the borrower of the securities. Further revenues should result from the lender's successfully applied strategy.

The costs of the lender are manifold, but not all of them have to be incurred.

IT and monitoring costs exist permanently. They are the compensation for the realisation of the securities lending transaction. Without electronic systems and continuous monitoring, securities lending cannot be carried out. Transaction costs of securities lending are also incurred (see Schmidt 1988, p. 7). These become visible when a bank steps between the lender and the borrower and demands a share of the premium for this service as an intermediary. Opportunity costs of the lender can also arise when securities are lent in t instead of sold. If the lender receives the securities back in T at lower prices, the lender realises a loss on a sale in T compared to an alternative sale in t (see Limmert 1994, p. 30).

Transaction costs are incurred at the chosen trading platform. However, the increasing supply ensures that the costs fall steadily and the transaction duration shorten (see Rettberg 2009, p. 20, Sommer 2014, pp. 6–7).

Risks arise for the lender in different forms. Individual risks exist at all times, while other risks occur only rarely or are even negligible.

There is always a liquidation risk of the collateral for the lender if the borrower defaults and can no longer fulfil his obligations. The liquidation of the collateral may take several days, which can result in opportunity losses for the lender. The proximity of the collateral to the money and a sufficient amount of collateral are important here. Liquidation risk exists if the securities lending agreement allows for early termination of the securities lending.

The credit risk seems to be relevant only in the case of securities lending without collateral, since no cash or securities admitted as collateral are provided. Defaults of the borrower or even the intermediaries may then have to be borne entirely by the lender or the intermediaries (see Jensen and Scheetz 1997, pp. 87–88, Jacklin and Felsenthal 1997, pp. 111–112).

The interest rate risk results from the extent of the lending period. Here a risk analysis and hedge of the collateral received is advisable, especially cash collateral (see Caan 1997, pp. 78–79). The interest rate risk and currency risk in cross-border securities lending exist permanently. Since market participants can hedge against these risks, they are not discussed further here.

3.1.3.2 Borrower

The borrower does not directly earn any revenues from securities lending. They come from the trading strategy of the borrower, if this has a positive course.

The costs of the borrower and the lender are comparable. The premium of the lender is the lending fee of the borrower, possibly reduced by the commission or the share of the intermediary.

Similar risks arise for the borrower and the lender. The borrower also bears a liquidation risk if the lender defaults and cannot return the collateral received, cash collateral or other long positions in securities to the borrower at the end of the loan. The borrower then has to sell the securities borrowed and may realise a loss if prices fall in the meantime. However, this liquidation risk is generally negligible in the case of institutionalised securities lending via the DKV or the lending system of the German banks.

The borrower is exposed to price risk if the prices of the securities change to the disadvantage of his strategy and he has to buy back the securities on the market at a loss (see Homm and Dag 2017, pp. 17–28, Janowski 2017, pp. 68–71).

A purchase risk exists if the liquidity of the borrowed securities is low. It may then happen that the securities borrowed and sold in t cannot be acquired on the market in T or can only be acquired with difficulty.

Operational risks and contractual risks also exist for the borrower, but these should be negligible in institutionalised securities lending.

3.1.3.3 Intermediaries

Intermediaries generate their revenues from commissions received and from interest income. These depend on the respective method of intermediation.

Costs arise for intermediaries from operational circumstances, e.g. the costs of operating procedures or monitoring costs. Costs can also arise if an intermediary has to take the place of a defaulting counterparty.

The risks of intermediaries differ only slightly from those of distributors and borrowers. Particularly noticeable is the risk of matching maturities in the intermediation of transactions, as can occur with the principal method.

The collateral of the intermediaries corresponds to that of the lenders and borrowers. Depending on the respective contract and position, money or securities are always provided as collateral.

Again, revenues and costs as well as risks and collateral of the market participants can be presented in Fig. 3.5.

3.2 Repos

3.2.1 Definition, Basic Form and Special Forms

In a normal repo, one market participant sells securities to another market participant (see Choudhry 2006, pp. 93–99, Cahn and Ostler 2008, pp. 4–5). Both agree at the same time that the seller will buy back these securities at the end of the repo term, at an initially agreed price (Miller 1997, p. 15). When repurchasing, the market participant pays the repo rate in addition to the purchase price. This is usually close to the money market interest rate for comparable maturities among partners

Fig. 3.5 Different revenues and costs as well as risks and collateral of the market participants

Revenues/Costs Risks/Securities	Lender	Borrower	Intermediary
Revenues from premium income	X		(X)
Transaction costs	X	X	(X)
Monitoring costs	X	X	(X)
Opportunity costs	X	X	
Premium payment costs		X	
Interest rate, currency and credit risk	(X)	(X)	(X)
Liquidation risk (maturity-dependent)	X	X	(X)
Collateral Securities	X		(X)
Collateral Cash position	X		(X)
Abondament of collateral	(X)	(X)	(X)

of first credit standing. This circumstance is significant because the fee for the securities lending described in the above section is usually only between 0.15% and 1.5% of the value of the securities bought or lent. Historically, it is in most cases below the interest rate for comparable maturities in the money market, which are relevant for repos. Payments can be made in T, but they can also be made in discounted form in t.

Traders also say that securities are lent and money is loaned (see Brooks 1996, pp. 2–4, Fabozzi and Mann 2005, pp. 226–233). The buyer provides collateral in money or securities, depending on the contract.

As with securities lending, a normal repo transaction can be illustrated in Fig. 3.6 (see Adrian et al. 2011, pp. 2–3).

In a reverse repo, the procedure is exactly the opposite. A market participant buys a security from another market participant. At the same time, the subsequent sale to the old owner of the security is agreed at a defined time and price. Traders also say that securities are lent and money is borrowed in a reverse repo. The proximity to securities lending is clear, where, from the perspective of the borrower, securities are lent and money is deposited in the form of collateral (Fabozzi and Jacobowitz 1997, pp. 189–199; McCrary 2012, pp. 120–122). The interest rate is usually passed on ex ante as a discount. The price at purchase in t is lower than the price at repurchase in T. The starting point of the transactions is the lending or purchase of the security (o.V. 2010, p. 33; McCrary 2012, pp. 116–118) (Fig. 3.7).

This is also close to a securities loan. Here, the bank takes securities as collateral and lends financial means. Interest is charged on these funds in the same way as on other bank loans.

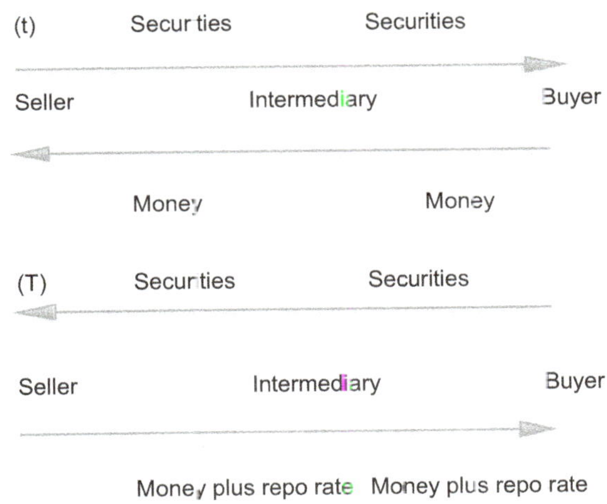

Fig. 3.6 Normal repo transactions with intermediary and Repo rate in T

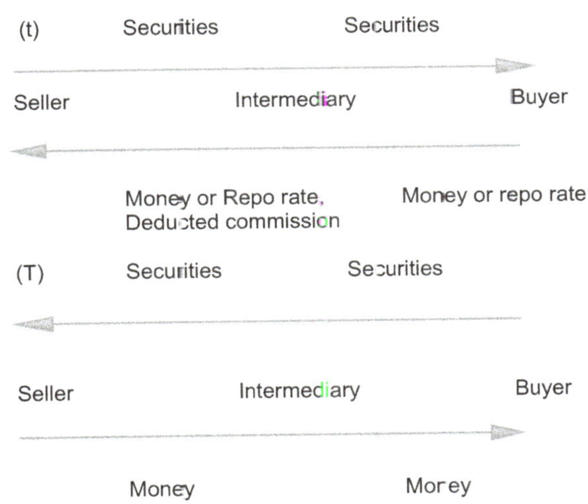

Fig. 3.7 Reverse repo with intermediary and discounted repo rate in t

Another form of a repo is a purchase/sale (or sale/purchase) in which both transactions and a future payment are fixed ex ante. The forward sale (or purchase) is comparable to an investment in a security in the money market. The payments are only made in T and are not to be accounted for by a discounted purchase price in t. A similarity to securities lending is clear here from the point of view of the lender, who receives the premiums/interest (see Faulkner 2005, pp. 11–12, Leez 2007, p. IX).

The positions in normal repo and reverse repo can be shown in Fig. 3.8.

The legal basis for repos is the German Commercial Code (HGB) and the trading regulations on the respective markets. Special trading regulations are not presented here in order to keep the scope of this work short.

Repos are divided into classical forms and special forms.

Normal repo (exchange purchase price plus repo rate in T)		
	Lender WP	Borrower WP
t	-WP + S	+WP = S
T	+WP - S * $(1+r)^{(T-t)}$	-WP = S * $(1+r)^{(T-t)}$ (Result equals result of securities lending!)

Reverse repo (discounted purchase price in t)		
	Borrower WP	Lender WP
t	+WP - S * $(1+r)^{-(T-t)}$	-WP = S * $(1+r)^{-(T-t)}$ (Result equals discounted result of securities lending)
T	-WP + S	+WP = S

Fig. 3.8 Payment flows from of Normal Repo and Reverse Repo

In the case of letter repos or hold-in-custody repos, the seller receives the money from the buyer. However, he continues to hold the securities serving as collateral in his own portfolio and does not have to deliver them. This is a one-sided transaction. These "trust me repos" are booked into a separate account of the trader to enable imputability (see also o.V. 1995, pp. 27–28). Letter repos are used when the collateral cannot be delivered or is small, but otherwise the costs associated with delivery would be high.

Letter repos or hold-in-custody repos have parallels to uncovered securities lending. The market participants do not have the securities lent in their inventory, the subsequent delivery is agreed individually. The similarities between securities lending and repos thus become particularly clear. The parallels can be illustrated in Fig. 3.9.

In delivery repos, according to their name, securities are delivered against money. This form of repo is similar to the simple basic form of repo. A characteristic feature is the daily revaluation of the individual positions in the securities and in the collateral, the mark-to-market. The first-ranking valuation of the collateral is prominent, not that of the entire repo (Miller 1997, pp. 23–24).

Other delivery repos are cross-currency repos based on different currencies, e.g. in securities delivered, collateral received or money paid (see Choudhry 2006, pp. 114–121). Similarities to swaps are clear (see Miller 1997, pp. 26–27).

The agent method is similar to securities lending with an intermediary. Again, an intermediary steps between buyer and seller (see Choudhry 2006, pp. 109–111, 313). He takes over securities and any collateral, and he supervises the payments (Burke and Martello 1997, p. 9; DÀmario 1997, p. 32; Choudhry 2006, pp. 123–126). Securities and payments are only booked and not actually delivered. This regularly increases the size and speed of repos.

Repo		
t	Lender	Borrower
		-> WP -> charged off account borrower <- Money (not discounted here)
T		<- WP -> Money + Repo rate
Securities lending		
T	Lender	Borrower
		-> WP <- Money
T		<- WP -> Money + WPL rate

Fig. 3.9 Parallels between repos and uncovered securities lending

In this paper, only normal and reverse repos are considered. A description of other repos is not intended.

3.2.2 *Market Participants and Motives*

The motives for trading in repos and the respective proceeds and costs as well as the risks and collateral are described below.

3.2.2.1 Pledgor

Repos are used by pledgers as risk management instruments. The market participant can take up a position for a certain point in time (e.g. on the balance sheet date). He can give it up again a short time later without incurring large costs or the risk of price changes. He can also simply close long positions without terminating them definitively if he considers the position to be overvalued.

Repos also help to cover certain short positions, here short in a stock, long in the money and investing the money in the repo (money) market for a short time. The market participant thus holds positions on both sides of a repo transaction, the entire position is closed.

If the market participant is long in a stock and short in the money, repos increase the returns or reduce the financing costs of a position on the money or capital market. He sells the stock in t and invests the proceeds in the money. In T, he buys back the stock and receives the investment of the proceeds in the money market. The interest payments received thus increase the return from the position in the stock or reduce the financing costs of the long position in the stock (Choudhry 2006, pp. 129–131).

3.2.2.2 Pledgee

The pledgee uses repos to manage risk. By accepting securities, the composition and risk structure of his portfolio changes. According to portfolio theory, he can thus increase or decrease his risk. By accepting a security as collateral and issuing money, the long position in money changes. Repos thus serve the pledgee to cover a long position in the money.

The increase in income through repos is another motive, in this case through the repo rate received for the accepted pledge. Another motive is a repo as an alternative to securities lending in order to reduce costs.

3.2.2.3 Intermediaries

The motives of intermediaries are to generate income from their intermediation activities. They will not be discussed further here.

3.2.3 Proceeds and Costs, Risks and Collateral

Repos generate different revenues and costs from the individual positions of the respective repos. These include risks that are reduced with contractually required collateral. These points are examined below for the individual market participants (see Limmert 1994, p. 3, Fabozzi and Jacobowitz 1997, pp. 195–199).

3.2.3.1 Pledgor

The generation of revenue is essential for pledgers. They accept money in order to invest it profitably, according to their respective motives. The proceeds from the related transactions should in aggregate be higher than the repo rate to be paid by the pledgor.

The formula for the success of a Normal Repo can be shown in formula 4.1.

Formula 4.1 : Success of the Normal Repo :

$$-WP + WP^{*}\ (1 + r_{REPO})^{(T\text{-}t)} > 0.$$

The success of a reverse repo is shown in Formula 4.2.

Formula 4.2 : Success of a Reverse Repo :

$$-WP^* \ (1 + r_{REPO})^{-(T-t)} + WP > 0$$

Another motive for repos is the avoidance of fees in alternative securities lending (see o.V. 2004, pp. 12–13).

Repos are fraught with risks that are limited by defined trading procedures and trading contracts (Benders 2006, p. 111).

Many risks of repos are comparable to those of securities lending. They are price risk, interest rate risk, currency risk, liquidity risk, organisational process risk and monitoring risk.

However, the counterparty risk, the risk of default of the business partner, receives the most attention (see Brooks 1995, pp. 10–11). Repos usually take place between two counterparties. The default of a market participant forces the remaining partner to close the open position, which is regularly associated with unforeseen costs. It is therefore all the more important to monitor the counterparty and to control the risk associated with it. The pledgor assumes the credit risk in a loan in kind, whereas the pledgee assumes the credit risk in the security (Oechler 1992, p. 569).

3.2.3.2 Pledgee

The pledgor generates income from his motives and strategies. The pledgee issues money and accepts securities as collateral. In The returns the securities and receives the money in return, plus the repo rate to be paid ex ante or ex post. It is essential that he receives both the proceeds from the transactions and the repo rate.

For the pledgee, the repo is also a cost-effective alternative to securities lending. The motive here is to reduce costs and increase income through lower costs.

The risks of the pledgee in a repo correspond to those of the pledgor. The same applies in particular to the counterparty risk and the credit risk.

3.2.3.3 Intermediaries

The proceeds and costs as well as the risks and collateral are again comparable with those of securities lending. Special features will not be explicitly described in the following.

The revenues and costs as well as the risks and collateral can be presented in a table for the different market participants. See Fig. 3.10.

Collateral is again provided for all market participants either as money or as securities, depending on the respective contracts.

Fig. 3.10 Revenues and costs as well as risks and collateral in the case of repos

	Pledgor	Pledgee	Intermediary
Proceeds from strategy with repo by repo rate	X	X	(X)
Cost reduction through repo instead of WPL	X	X	
Risks as with WPL, but especially counterparty risk	X	X	(X)
Collateral	X	X	(X)

Fig. 3.11 Comparison of securities lending and repos

Comparable features	Securities lending and repo	Comment
Legal structure	different	Different legal treatment
Lending premium and repo rate	different	Different heights and dates
Intermediary	Partly similar	
Motifs	similar to	
Collateral	similar to	
Costs	very similar	
Risks	very similar	

3.3 Comparison of Securities Lending and Repos and Discussion of Assumptions

3.3.1 Comparison of Securities Lending and Repos

It is clear that securities lending and repos are different instruments that have much in common (see Adrian et al. 2011, p. 2) (Fig. 3.11).

There are some special features that should be mentioned: In the case of a simple repo, the proximity to securities lending is clear, where, from the lender's point of view, securities are sold at the beginning and money is deposited in the form of collateral. At repurchase, the purchase price plus the repo rate is paid. The transfer of the securities is the essential starting point of the transactions.

A reverse repo is also close to a securities loan. Here, securities are taken as collateral by the bank and financial resources are lent. Interest is charged on these funds in the same way as on other loans.

Letter repos or hold-in-custody repos have great similarities to uncovered securities lending. In these, the market participants do not hold the lent securities in inventory, the subsequent delivery is only agreed off-exchange. The similarities between securities lending and repos become particularly clear here.

3.3.2 Discussion of Assumptions

This paper shows securities lending and repos on the financial markets of the Federal Republic of Germany. This requires assumptions about the conditions on the financial markets.

The assumptions are presented below and compared with reality. Deviations are to be shown and their effects on securities lending and repos in Germany analysed (see also Hohmann 1996, pp. 20–22, Faulkner 2005, pp. 7–8).

1. Arbitrage-free markets exist, all required instruments are traded there, the actual prices always correspond to the theoretical values.

   This assumption is not entirely true. All instruments are not traded at all times, arbitrage opportunities also exist. However, if the required instruments are not traded, market participants can substitute them by duplication or simply neglect them. The mispricing of derivative instruments is of less relevance for the strategies to be shown. They aim at arbitrage with securities lending, repos and derivatives. The remoteness from reality of assumption 1. is to be tolerated in the following.
2. Market participants invest in financial securities on the markets and want to maximise their benefit.

   This assumption should be given.
3. There are no dividend payments or changes in capital.

   Dividends are usually paid and capital changes can also be made. However, these are less relevant for securities lending and repos, as the payment of dividends and changes in capital are regulated in the contracts between the market participants involved.
4. There is only one currency, borrowing and investment of funds at a positive credit-risk-free interest rate is possible, there is a constant horizontal yield curve. There are no taxes.

   There are several currencies in the world, but in Germany the value date is in euros. In the following, only strategies in Germany are presented; the foreign exchange market and related strategies are not observed.

   In reality, borrowing and investing at the credit-risk-free interest rate is possible for the Bundesbank; market participants can only invest in credit-risk-free securities of the Federal Government in this particular case (see Schmidt 1979, p. 711, Schmidt 1981, pp. 249–286). If the credit-risk-free interest rate is negative, as it was currently the case on some European markets, the realisation of strategies with securities lending and repos is more difficult. This circumstance will not last forever and is contrary to all experience. With a view to normal conditions in the future, it is negligible.

   Usually, there is no constant and horizontal yield curve. This circumstance is insignificant for strategies with securities lending and repos, since there are regularly no position changes during the term of the strategies.

   The situation is different for strategies with options and futures. If the relevant interest rate changes significantly, the price of the forward market instrument changes, even if other market conditions remain constant. The price of the futures market instrument in T then differs from that calculated in t. The success of the strategy then differs from that calculated in t too. The success of the strategy then deviates from the desired result. In the following, it is assumed that the terms of the strategies are only short and therefore the effects of changing interest rates are limited.

In reality, taxes have to be paid. However, they are usually incurred ex post for the above transactions. Taxes should not be relevant for ex ante planning and then execution of the strategies.

5. Share prices follow a log-normally distributed process at the end of a time interval.

   In reality, share prices rarely follow a log-normally distributed process. There are different price distributions; instead of a discrete course, the price courses can show jumps. Even with the inclusion of overseas markets, stock exchange trading does not take place for 24 h.

   The impact of price jumps on strategies with cash market instruments is limited, as market participants hold closed positions. The situation is different for strategies with futures market instruments. Price jumps can abruptly change the prices of futures market instruments without a simultaneous adjustment of the portfolio. Despite closed positions in t, the result in T then deviates from the target value.

   How big the effects of price jumps are will be shown by the application of the strategies in reality. This question remains unanswered here.

6. The volatility of share prices and returns is known and constant.

   The volatility of share prices and returns is not known or constant. For strategies with cash market instruments, the effects are small because market participants usually hold closed positions. The situation is different for strategies with securities lending and repos with futures market instruments. Temporarily changed volatilities change the prices of options, even if other market conditions remain constant. The adjustment to changed volatilities must be made to the appropriate extent, despite closed positions in t, otherwise the result in T deviates from the target value.

   The effect of volatilities that have changed in the meantime will be shown by the application of the strategies in reality. This question is not to be dealt with here.

7. Transaction costs do not exist.

   This assumption is unrealistic. In financial markets, services are rendered that have to be remunerated. Transaction costs consist of pagatorial and calculatory components. These are the costs of the transaction service of the bank or the intermediary, the transaction-related information and decision costs, the costs of hedging against transaction risks and the costs of immediate closing.

   If market participants want to trade shares on stock exchanges in Germany, they have to pay a commission to the trading partner. This is included in the share price as a premium or implicitly as a mark-up or deduction. This commission varies in amount, depending on the market depth, liquidity and size of the order. It ranges from zero to EUR 4.95 per trade in the case of electronic banks to several percent of the price of the traded position in the case of unfavourable trading conditions.

If market participants want to trade interest-bearing securities in Germany, they also have to pay a commission. In internet exchanges these costs amount to a few per mille of the nominal value of the traded securities, but in the case of unfavourable trading conditions in hardly liquid securities they can be many times higher.

When trading in futures market instruments, the transaction costs can usually be significantly lower than when trading in comparable positions on the cash market. In times of low volatility, according to practical experience, 10% of the costs are to be paid by the cash market, but in times of high or extreme volatility, the transaction costs for futures market instruments can increase significantly. The exact amount cannot be predicted ex ante. In this paper, transaction costs are not emphasised in the presentation of strategies.

Transaction costs make the duplication of futures market instruments and their valuation difficult (see Hohmann 1996, p. 212). In the strategies shown here, transactions take place in t and, if necessary, in T. Transaction costs can then influence the result planned in t and achieved in T. It is not possible to apply the strategies at all. This does not make the application of the strategies completely impossible.

8. The strategies with securities lending and repos have no significant influence on price developments.

   This assumption should be correct. It cannot be seen how strategies with securities lending and repos and spot market and/or futures market instruments, which are unknown up to now, can significantly influence prices. Nor is it possible to see how securities lending and repos would be decisive for price movements during the financial crisis in 2001, 2007–2009 or 2020.

9. All maturities for tradable securities are given in the market and the securities are divisible.

   This assumption does not hold. Market participants should then substitute securities again or choose other maturities to pursue their strategies. They can also choose a roll-over strategy with short-dated contracts on the futures market. In this case, however, they have to bear higher transaction costs.

   If the securities are not divisible, the market participants can increase the size of the positions until they can realise the desired strategy. There is a maximum proportion of securities to be lent in individual classes, which makes securities lending more difficult. Early termination by the lender may also be possible. However, maximum amount and termination are not to be taken into account for the strategies to be shown.

10. Market participants act rationally, simultaneous trading is always given. There are no market entry restrictions, market participants do not have to provide collateral. There are no taxes, balance sheet regulations or restrictive legal provisions.

This assumption is problematic. If market participants always acted proportionally, there would not have been some price distortions in the recent past. However, this question is not essential for the strategies to be shown, as it has no impact on them.

Simultaneous trading of all instruments is not always the case. Within the framework of the strategies, however, the market participants open a position in t, which they subsequently close in T. The simultaneous trading of all instruments is not always the case. Questions of simultaneous trading are therefore of less interest.

Market entry restrictions exist. They result from legal trading restrictions for selected market participants. These are therefore taken as given in the following. The same applies to trade barriers due to taxation and accounting regulations.

Market participants must also provide collateral. This is necessary for mark-to-the-market on the derivatives markets, as well as for strategies with securities lending and repos.

Assumption 10 is unrealistic, but it is not essential for the strategies to be shown.

11. No interim payments are made from the collateral.

    This assumption does not apply. In reality, payments such as interest or dividends always have to be interest-bearing or discounted.

12. Only European options exist.

    This assumption is incorrect; in reality, American options and combinations of both option types exist. In the following, strategies with European options are presented, the differences in the application with American options are pointed out.

    What stands out in the multitude of assumptions is that there are transaction costs contrary to the assumptions. This circumstance is to be examined in particular in the following in order to assess the application of the strategies in practice.

Chapter 4
Strategies with Securities Lending and Repos

Selected strategies with securities lending, with repos or with both are presented below. The assumptions stated apply again. Additional assumptions are included where appropriate.

Strategies with securities lending and futures contracts on equities and equity indices are presented first. Strategies with options on equities and equity indices follow.

The procedure for strategies with repos is the same.

Finally, strategies combining securities lending and repos on different underlying securities are shown.

A limitation to equities, futures and options is given here. Strategies with other equity securities or strategies with interest-bearing securities on the cash and futures market are possible. However, these cannot be dealt with within the scope of this work.

A distinction between on-exchange and off-exchange derivatives is neglected. Off-exchange creditworthiness or transaction risks can be hedged individually by the market participant.

The objective of all strategies to be shown is always that $r_i > r_f$, with no or equal risk.

4.1 Securities Lending with Futures Contracts on Stocks and Stock Indices

In the following strategy, the market participant uses one or more stocks, stock indices and securities lending as instruments. The market participant pursues the approach of differential arbitrage. He wants to profit from a temporary situation on the market in order to achieve an excess return. He takes a closed position, the possibility of losses from the strategy theoretically does not exist.

R. Hohmann, *Securities Lending and Repos*, SpringerBriefs in Finance,
https://doi.org/10.1007/978-3-658-41984-4_4

For simplification, the assumption is now that futures contracts on the desired stocks, individually or as an index, are traded. Corresponding to the valuation of futures on stocks or stock indices (see Kolb 1991, p. 424, Hull 1993, pp. 51–52), formula 5 applies to the valuation of a future in t.

Formula 5 for the valuation of a stock futures contact:

$$\text{Formula 5}: F_t = S_t{}^{*}\ (1 + r_f)^{(T\text{-}t)}$$
$$\Rightarrow 0 = S_t{}^{*}\ (1 + r_f)^{(T\text{-}t)}\text{-}Ft$$

with

F_t = price of a future in t
S_t = Price of a stock in t

The formula does not include the opportunity of securities lending.

We will now show the strategy in which the market participant has a long position in a stock in t. He sells it in t via a forward. He sells it in t via a futures contract with delivery in T. Here the simplifying assumption applies that no payments flow from the sale in t, these are only offset in T with the cash settlement. (In reality, however, payments are made in t, and questions of the compounding and discounting rate then arise in contradiction to assumption 11. In the case of extremely low or negative interest rates, as have existed for years, the contradiction here is justifiable). At the same time, the market participant in t lends out the stock he holds long for the period (T − t). This procedure in t can be formally represented as follows:

$$+S_t\text{-}S_t{}^{*}\ (1 + r_f)^{(T\text{-}t)}\text{-}S_{t,WPL} = 0$$

with $S_{t,\ WPL}$ = price of a stock that is lent or borrowed via a securities lending

At the end of the securities lending in T, the market participant receives the stock back plus the lending premium for the period (T − t). He uses the received stock to settle his obligation from the sale of the futures contract in cash. He can either deliver the stock or he can sell it and fulfil the cash settlement with the financial means received. In this way, he can offset losses or realise profits. He also has the premium from the sale of the future in t at his disposal. This procedure in T can be formally represented as follows:

$$+S_T + S_t{}^{*}\ r_{WPL}{}^{(T\text{-}t)}\text{-}S_T + S_t{}^{*}r_f{}^{(T\text{-}t)} > 0$$

with r_{WPL} = rate of return from securities lending/lending fee or premium

In T is the result of this strategy:

$$S_t{}^* \; r_f{}^{(T\text{-}t)} + S_t{}^* \; r_{WPL}{}^{(T\text{-}t)}$$
$$\Rightarrow S_t{}^* \; (1 + r_f + r_{WPL})^{(T\text{-}t)} > S_t{}^* \; (1 + r_f)^{(T\text{-}t)}$$

This then results in the new formula 4.1 for the valuation of stock futures.

$$\text{Formula 4.1}: F_t = S_t{}^* \; (1 + r_f + r_{WPL})^{(T\text{-}t)}$$

The procedure shown applies not only to individual shares but also to portfolios of shares, for example in an index. In this case, too, the market participant achieves an excess return, which is not shown again (see Hohmann 1991, p. 580).

Naked short selling, the uncovered short selling of a position on the cash market, which can be attributed to securities lending, is interesting. This is to be compared with a short sale of a future in t. The lending fee is then paid in T, but no opportunity interest is taken into account in the future price. If the lender does not take this circumstance into account in the required lending premiums, which are then increased in the case of positive interest rates, he leaves the opportunity interest to the borrower of the securities free of charge.

Excursus: Strategy with long cash and borrowing in t.

Here the market participant initially has a long position in the money in t. The size of the position corresponds to the price of a stock in t. The market participant invests this money at interest for the time period (T − t). He can borrow the stock simultaneously for the same period. The invested money then serves as collateral. Borrowing the stock is an option that is not mandatory. The procedure can be formally represented with:

$$(+V)\text{-}V \; (+S) = 0, \text{with } V = S \text{ in t}$$

with V = value of the asset in T, measured in the price of the asset.

In T the market participant again holds his position in the money. The invested asset has been repaid plus interest. If he borrowed the share in t, he returns the share in T, plus the lending fee for the corresponding period. The formal representation is now as follows:

$$(+V) + V^* \; r_f{}^{(T\text{-}t)}\text{-}S^* \; (1 - r_{WPL})^{(T\text{-}t)} > 0$$

In T is the result of this strategy:

$$V^* \; (1 + r_f)^{(T\text{-}t)}\text{-}S^* \; (1 + r_{WPL})^{(T\text{-}t)} > 0, \text{with } r_f > r_{WPL}$$

With the above strategy, the market participant achieves a return that corresponds to the risk-free interest rate for a comparable term. However, if he has borrowed the share for the corresponding period, the result is reduced by the lending fee to be paid. The return is only positive if $r_f > r_{WPL}$. It is now also of interest whether the payment dates for r_f and r_{WPL} fall on the same date. Due to diverging payment dates, risks such as the interest rate risk or the counterparty risk can occur and influence the result of the strategy.

The strategy with long cash and borrowing in t is suboptimal. It leads to a deterioration of the results compared to the previous strategy. It will be neglected in the following.

4.2 Securities Lending with Options on Shares and Share Indices

The market participant wants to achieve a return with options on stocks and stock indices through differential arbitrage. His position is closed, the risk of losses theoretically non-existent. Formula 6 for put-call parity applies to the valuation of European call and put options (see Cox and Rubinstein 1985, pp. 41–44):

$$\text{Formula 6}: P + S_t = C + K^* \ (1 + r_f)^{-(T\text{-}t)}, \text{ with } S_t = K$$
$$\Rightarrow S_t = C + K^* \left(1 + r_f\right)^{-(T\text{-}t)}\text{-}P \Rightarrow 0 = C + K^* \left(1 + r_f\right)^{-(T\text{-}t)}\text{-}P\text{-}S_t$$

In the case of American options, the opportunity to exercise the option at any time between t and T exists. With formula 6 otherwise the same, the call is then not to be discounted.

The opportunity to borrow securities is not included in formula 6 for European options. This circumstance is taken into account in the following procedure (See Hohmann 1992, pp. 160–163).

In t the market participant again has a long position in the stock. He lends the stock from his portfolio in t with maturity T. At the same time he buys a call on the stock, simultaneously sells a corresponding put and takes up financial resources in the amount of K^* $(1 + r_f)^{-(T - t)}$. Formally, this procedure can be represented as follows:

$$\text{-}S_{t,WPL} + C + K_t^* \ (1 + r_f)^{-(T\text{-}t)}\text{-}P = 0$$
$$\Rightarrow 0 = C\text{-}P + K_t^* \ (1 + r_f)^{-(T\text{-}t)}\text{-}S_{t,WPL}$$

In T the market participant receives the lent stock back, plus the lending premium for the period (T – t). The market participant is now long the stock. At the same time, he has to repay the funds borrowed in t. In return, he can sell the stock and repay the loan premium. To do so, he can sell the stock and use the proceeds, or he can use the stock as collateral for another financing. Furthermore, in T the opposing value developments of call and put compensate each other. The procedure is formally represented in formula 6.1:

$$\text{Formula 6.1}: S_t^* (1 + r_{WPL})^{(T\text{-}t)}\text{-}C\text{-}K + P > 0$$
$$\Rightarrow S_t^* \, r_{WPL}{}^{(T\text{-}t)} > 0$$

The market participant thus achieves a return that is above the risk-free interest rate for corresponding maturities. The risk of loss of value of the position in (T − t) is theoretically non-existent. The same procedure is also possible for an equity portfolio.

4.3 Repos with Futures Contracts on Stocks and Stock Indices

In the following strategy, the market participant uses repos and again stocks and/or stock indices and futures contracts on them. Here, too, he follows the principle of differential arbitrage in order to achieve an excess return from a closed position.

The same assumptions apply as for securities lending with stocks and/or stock indices and the corresponding futures contracts. Assume that payments from a position in a repo are only payable in T, not t.

Again, formula 5 applies to the value of a future in t.

$$\text{Formula 5}: F_t = S_t^* (1 + r_f)^{(T\text{-}t)}$$
$$\Rightarrow 0 = S_t^* (1 + r_f)^{(T\text{-}t)}\text{-}F_t$$

Repos are not included in the formula. Their benefit is to be shown in the following.

In t the market participant has a long position in a stock. He sells a futures contract on this stock. Assuming that no payments flow from the sale, these are only offset in T with the cash settlement. (Payments to be made in T are usually discounted to t. Here they are accrued from t to T. Here they are compounded from t to T. The relative size of the payments, measured in percent, remains the same, only the absolute size, measured in payment units, changes. The difference is not relevant for the following illustrations; any inaccuracies should be tolerable). At the same time, he also sells the stock via a repo. Positions and payment flows can be represented as follows:

$$+S_t\text{-}S_t^* (1 + r_f)^{(T\text{-}t)}\text{-}S_{t,Repo} = 0$$

with $S_{t,\,REPO}$ = price of a stock in t that is bought or sold via a repo. sold

In T, the market participant receives the stock back from the repo. He also receives the repo rate for the period (T − t). With the stock, he fulfils his obligation from the sale of the futures contract via the cash settlement. Exceptionally, he can deliver the stock, or he can sell it and make the cash settlement with the funds received. He also receives, or still has at his disposal, the premium from the sale of the future in t. Formally, this procedure is to be represented in T as follows:

$$+S_T + S_t{}^* \, r_{Repo}{}^{(T\text{-}t)} \text{-} S_T + S_t{}^* \, r_f{}^{(T\text{-}t)} > 0$$

with r_{Repo} = rate of return from a repo/repo rate.

The result of this strategy is:

$$S_t{}^* \, r_{Repo}{}^{(T\text{-}t)} + S_t{}^* \, r_f{}^{(T\text{-}t)} > S_t{}^* \, r_f{}^{(Tst)}$$

Formula 5.2 for equity futures valuation with repos now reads:

$$\text{Formula 5.2}: F_t = S_t{}^* \left(1 + r_f + r_{Repo}\right)^{(T\text{-}t)}$$

It is obvious that this procedure does not only apply to individual stocks, but also to portfolios of stocks, e.g. of a stock index. A description of this will be omitted here.

4.4 Repos with Options on Shares and Share Indices

Here, too, the market participant uses differential arbitrage to achieve an excess return. His position is closed, losses are theoretically excluded. For the valuation of European call and put options, formula 6 applies to the put-call parity:

$$\text{Formula 6}: P + S_t = C + K^* \, (1 + r_f)^{\text{-}(T\text{-}t)}, \text{with } S_t = K_t$$
$$\Rightarrow S_t = C + K^* \left(1 + r_f\right)^{-(T-t)} - P \Rightarrow 0 = C + K^* \left(1 + r_f\right)^{\text{-}(T\text{-}t)} - P - S_t$$

The repo opportunity is not included in the formula. It is shown as follows. Again, the market participant has a long position in the stock. Via a normal repo he now sells the stock in t from his portfolio with maturity T. He buys a call on the stock, simultaneously sells a corresponding put and sells financial means in the amount of $K^* \, (1 + r_f)^{-(T-t)}$. It is assumed that all interest and repo rate payments are made only in T. Formally, this procedure is as follows:

$$\text{-}S_{t,Repo} + C + K^* \, (1 + r_f)^{-(T\text{-}t)} \text{-} P = 0$$
$$\Rightarrow 0 = C\text{-}P + K^* \, (1 + r_f)^{\text{-}(T\text{-}t)} - S_{t,Repo}$$

Here we should again refer to American options, where in the otherwise same formula 6 the call in t is not discounted.

For European options, the market participant receives the sold stock back in T, plus the repo rate for the period (T – t). The market participant is now long the stock

Fig. 4.1 Comparison of essential formulas of strategies with Futures contracts or options

Strategies with futures contracts	Strategies with options
Formula 5: $F_t = S_t * (1+r_f)^{(T-t)}$ with $F_t > 0$	Formula 6: $P + S_t = C + K * (1+r_f)^{-(T-t)}$
Formula 5.1: $F_t = S_t * (1+r_f+r_{WPL})^{(T-t)}$ with $F_t > 0$	Formula 6.1: $S_t * (1+r_{WPL})^{(T-t)} - C - K + P > 0$
Formula 5.2: $F_t = S_t * (1+r_f+ r_{Repo})^{(T-t}$ with $F_t > 0$	Formula 6.2: $S_t * (1+r_{Repo})^{(T-t)} - C - K + P > 0$

Fig. 4.2 Successes of the strategies

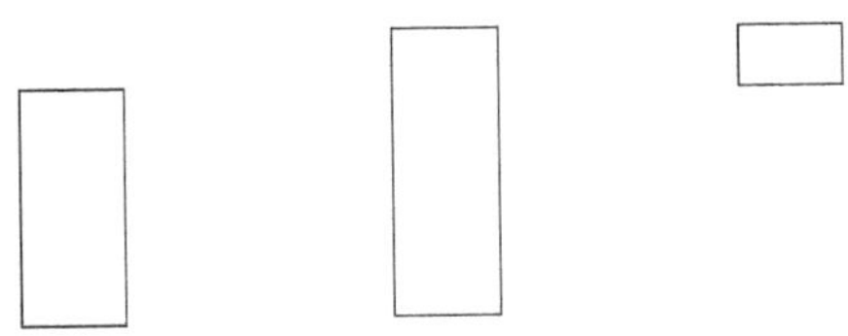

$- F_t$	$S_t * (1+r_f + r_{WPL})^{(T-t)}$	= Excess return Formula 4.1
- Ft	$S_t * (1+r_f + r_{Repo})^{(T-t)}$	= excess return Formula 4.2
- C - K	$S_t * (1+ r_{WPL})^{(T-t)}$	= Excess return Formula 5.1
- C - K	$S_t * (1+ r_{Repo})^{(T-t)}$	= excess return Formula 5.2

again. At the same time, he must buy back the funds sold in t. He can use the stock for this purpose by buying it back at the repo rate. To do this, he can use the stock by selling it and receiving financial resources, or he can use the stock as collateral for another financing. Again, in T the opposing value developments of call and put compensate each other. The procedure is formally represented as in formula 6.2:

$$\text{Formula 6.2}: S_t^* \left(1 + r_{Repo}\right)^{(T\text{-}t)} \text{-C-K} + P > 0$$
$$\Rightarrow S_t^* \, r_{Repo}{}^{(T\text{-}t)} > 0$$

The market participant thus again achieves an excess return that is above the risk-free interest rate for corresponding maturities. The risk of losses in the value of the position in (T – t) is theoretically excluded.

Sections 4.1–4.4 contain strategies with which market participants can achieve excess returns. The strategies can be presented in a formal comparison as in Fig. 4.1.

Figure 4.1 shows that in the formulas 5.1 and 5.2 as well as 6.1 and 6.2 only the rate of return for securities lending and repo is different. All other components of the formula are identical. This circumstance illustrates the economic proximity of securities lending and repos, despite differing legal definitions.

The success of the strategies can also be shown in a diagram. The main formulas are shown in Fig. 4.2.

4.5 Securities Lending with Repos and Vice Versa

In the following, strategies are shown that combine securities lending and repos. In this way, returns can be achieved that are above the risk-free interest rate for corresponding maturities. The key factor here is the level of the securities lending premium compared to the repo rate.

Strategies with securities lending and repos with stocks and stock index futures or stocks and stock index options are feasible. When viewed in isolation, these strategies already yield an excess return. The market participant should therefore choose the strategy, depending on the securities lending premium or repo rate, which yields the higher return. The market participant then applies compensatory arbitrage. It is interesting to note here that balancing arbitrage is theoretically not risk-free. However, the positions of the above strategies can be closed or hedged with additional derivatives, so there is no risk.

Difference arbitrage can also be used by the market participant, depending on the level of the securities lending premium and repo rate. If r_{WPL} is smaller or larger than r_{Repo}, the market participant lends or borrows the securities and buys or sells securities in the market accordingly. Formally, the positions of this procedure can be depicted as follows in Fig. 4.3.

The market participant can also use securities lending and repo in one position. He then has a long position in both instruments with the same maturity. The procedure here is as follows (see Hohmann 1995).

In t the market participant enters into a normal repo with an exchange purchase price. In return, he gives out financial resources, in this case money, and takes in securities as collateral. The market participant then lends out these securities, in this case stocks, for the same term as the repo.

The payment flows can be formally represented:

$$-V_{t,Repo} + S_t - S_{t,WPL} = 0;$$

with $V_t = S_t$, V_t = financial resources in t.

Fig. 4.3 Differential arbitrage with securities lending and repo

a) with $r_{WPL} > r_{Repo}$, $r_{WPL} - r_{REPO} > 0$

in t: $+ S_t - S_t = 0$

in T: $- S_t * (1+r_{Repo})^{(T-t)} + S_t * (1+r_{WPL})^{(T-t)} > 0$

b) with: $r_{Repo} > r_{WPL}$, $r_{Repo} - r_{WPL} > 0$

in t: $- S_t + S_t = 0$

in T: $+ S_t * (1+r_{Repo})^{(T-t)} - S_t * (1+r_{WPL})^{(T-t)} > 0$

In T at the end of the term, the market participant receives the lent securities back, plus the lending premium. At the same time, the repo ends and the market participant returns the securities received as collateral to the pledgor. He receives his financial resources back, in this case money, and also the agreed repo rate.

The procedure is formally illustrated in formula 7:

$$\text{Formula 7}: +S_{t,WPL}{}^{*}\ (1 + r_{WPL})^{(T\text{-}t)}\text{-}S_t + V_{t,Repo}{}^{*}\ (1 + r_{Repo})^{(T-t)} > 0$$

$$\Rightarrow S_t{}^{*}\ (1 + r_{WPL} + r_{Repo})^{(T\text{-}t)} > 0$$

The market participant achieves an excess return above the risk-free interest rate for comparable maturities. The result is similar to the result of strategies with securities lending or repos with stock index futures. Default risks should be negligible in standardised settlement organisations such as Deutscher Kassenver-ein or Clearstream/Eurex.

Chapter 5
Summary and Outlook

The above explanations show how excess returns can be achieved through strategies with securities lending and repos. The discussion of assumptions showed that the strategies can be implemented with few restrictions on German and probably also international money and capital markets. Selected states, however, require a more detailed consideration.

Returns from pledged collateral such as interest or dividends were not taken into account in the strategies. However, when applying the strategies in reality, these must be taken into account. It is important to know to whom the income accrues and how its organisational transfer is to be fulfilled. The effects of the income from collateral should be immediately obvious; a detailed presentation is dispensed with.

Transactions with securities lending and repos require substantial financial resources. According to practical experience, sums of between 300 million euros and 500 million euros are required. Institutional investors regularly have these funds at their disposal. They use securities lending and repos to increase their returns (see O.V 2013a, b, p. 2; o.V. 2020, pp. 1–27). The strategies shown above are mostly feasible without risk. Risk-free excess returns of 0.1–0.25% then lead to earnings of several million euros for institutional market participants.

Transaction costs always occur in practice. For most institutional market participants, transaction costs are between 0.05% and 0.15% of the value of the traded securities. The values are lower for interest-bearing securities and higher for equity securities. However, transaction costs should generally not be higher than the lowest premium rate for securities lending of 0.1% to 0.25%, and not higher at all for premium rates of 0.5% to 0.75%. Transaction costs therefore do not prevent the feasibility of strategies with securities lending.

Transaction costs can, however, prevent the use of strategies with repos in individual cases. The repo rate is often close to the risk-free interest rate for comparable maturities. With a very low or even negative risk-free interest rate, the strategies with repos are then hardly or not at all realisable due to the comparatively higher transaction costs.

R. Hohmann, *Securities Lending and Repos*, SpringerBriefs in Finance,
https://doi.org/10.1007/978-3-658-41984-4_5

Transaction costs are in most cases below the rates of the securities lending premium or repo rate. According to the realism of the previously discussed assumptions, the realisation of strategies with securities lending and with repos should be possible in practice. This circumstance seems clear. Empirical analysis of the effects of transaction costs on the results of the strategies can therefore be dispensed with here. Another obstacle to such an empirical analysis is that historical data on securities lending premiums and repo rates are not available.

Market participants can achieve excess returns with the strategies shown, but the positions built up should be risk-free. The significance and consequences of these results were discussed in conclusion.

The application of the strategy in practice is to be expected. As shown at the beginning of this paper, securities lending and repos have been subject to unjustified criticism. However, the comments have recently become more objective and positive. A broader application of the above strategies with securities lending and repos will take place, and the overall economic benefit will then accrue to all market participants, as well as to those who do not participate in this particular market.

Chapter 6
Epilogue

In this paper, strategies with securities lending and repos have been presented. Further thoughts on this subject suggest themselves.

It is not conclusively clear why securities lending and repos have different relative lending premiums and repo rates, although they are economically comparable. One explanation for this could lie in property rights. The valuation of property could be a relevant variable for this. Here lies an approach to research in the future.

Options are valued via the put-call parity. As mentioned above, there is an opportunity to achieve an excess return. Securities lending and repos should then be embedded in the option valuation shown. The same applies to other valuation theories, such as the duplication of options or the model of Black and Scholes and its further developments.

With the strategies presented, market participants can achieve excess returns, regardless of the level of the risk-free interest rate. They can realise it with securities lending at a risk-free interest rate that is both above or below the rate for the lending premium, or at a negative interest rate, as in the recent past. However, if the risk-free rate is no longer sufficiently relevant, the question is how important it is as a price for lending money or even capital. The answer to this question is reserved for future work.

R. Hohmann, *Securities Lending and Repos*, SpringerBriefs in Finance,
https://doi.org/10.1007/978-3-658-41984-4_6

Bibliography

Adrian T, Begalle B, Copeland A, Martin A (2011) Working Paper - Repo and securities lending, o. O., 2011

Benders R (2006) Stock exchange lowers repo fee, in HB, No. 94, 16.5.2006, p 111

Blitz J, Illhardt J (1990) Wertpapierleihe beim Deutschen Kassenverein. Die Bank 3(1990): 142–149

Brooks A (1995) Orange Blues, in Repo, a RISK REPO supplement, November 1995, pp 10–13

Brooks A (1996) Equity Repo comes of age. Risk 9(10):2–3

Burke K, Martello G (1997) The evolution of securities lending. In: Fabozzi FJ (ed) Securities lending and repurchase agreements. New Hope, Pennsylvania

Caan GW Jr (1997) Managing internal lending programs. In: Fabozzi FJ (ed) Securities lending and repurchase agreements. New Hope, Pennsylvania

Cahn A, Ostler N (2008). Own shares and securities lending. In Working Paper Series No. 76, ed. Institute For Law And Finance - Johann Wolfgang Goethe Universität-Frankfurt, 01/2008

Chichilinsky G (2012) Short sales and financial innovation: how to take the good while avoiding widespread default. In: Gregoriou GN (ed) Handbook of short selling. Elsevier, Oxford, pp 5–8

Choudhry M (2006) The REPO handbook, 1st edn - Reprinted 2004, 2006. Butterworth-Heinemann, Oxford

Cohen J, Haushalter D, Reed AV (2004) Mechanics of the equity lending market. In: Fabozzi FJ (ed) Short selling, strategies, risks, and rewards. Wiley, Hoboken, NJ

Cox JC, Rubinstein M (1985) Options markets. Prentice-Hall, Englewood Cliffs, NJ

DÀmario (1997) The nondollar repo market. In: Fabozzi FJ (ed) Securities lending and repurchase agreements. New Hope, Pennsylvania

Fabozzi FJ, Jacobowitz E (1997) Understanding cash collateral reinvestment risks. In: Fabozzi FJ (ed) Securities lending and repurchase agreements. New Hope, Pennsylvania

Fabozzi FJ, Mann SV (2005) Repurchase and reverse repurchase agreements. In: Fabozzi FJ, Mann SV (eds) Securities finance, securities lending and repurchase agreements. Wiley, Hoboken, NJ

Faulkner MC (2000). Securities lending and corporate governance, n.d.

Faulkner MC (2005) Finding a route to market: an institutional guide to the securities lending maze. In: Fabozzi FJ, Mann SV (eds) Securities finance, securities lending and re-purchase agreements. Wiley, Hoboken, NJ

Faulkner MC, Sackville CLS (1997) Finding a route to market: an institutional guide to the securities lending maze. In: Fabozzi FJ (ed) Securities lending and repurchase agreements. New Hope, Pennsylvania

Godek M (2001) Short selling as a strategy, in HB, No. 186, 26.9.2001, pp B11, B12

R. Hohmann, *Securities Lending and Repos*, SpringerBriefs in Finance,
https://doi.org/10.1007/978-3-658-41984-4

Häuselmann H, Wiesenbart T (1990) Die Bilanzierung und Besteuerung von Wertpapier-Leihgeschäften, in Wochenschrift für Betriebswirtschaft, Steuerrecht, Wirtschaftsrecht, Ar-beitsrecht, 43rd Jg, Heft 43

Heinke E (1992) The short-term surrender of papers opens up new sources of income for investors, in HB, No. 165, 27.8,1992, pp B 23-B 24

Hohmann R (1991) The influence of securities lending on the valuation of the DAX future, in KaRS Kapitalanlagen, No. 8/9, 1.9.1991, pp 574–582

Hohmann R (1992) Securities lending and put-call parity - a German free lunch? Die Bank 3(1992): 160–163

Hohmann R (1995) Making more profit with repurchase agreement and securities lending, in Blick durch die Wirtschaft, 17.11.1995

Hohmann R (1996) Portfolio insurance in Germany - strategies against share price losses. DUV. Dt. Univ.-Verl, Wiesbaden

Homm F and Dag G (2017) The art of short selling, ed. DIE ZWEITE MEINUNG GmbH, Hattersheim

Hull JC (1993) Options, futures, and other derivative securities, 2nd edn. Prentice Hall International Editions, Englewood Cliffs, NJ

Jacklin N, Felsenthal D (1997) International legal and regulatory concerns. In: Fabozzi FJ (ed) Securities lending and repurchase agreements. New Hope, Pennsylvania, pp 189–200

Janowski T (2017) Stock short selling with inverse ETFs, ed. AutorenServices.de, Fulda

Jensen MR, Scheetz RW (1997) Performance measurement for securities lending. In: Fabozzi FJ (ed) Securities lending and repurchase agreements. New Hope, Pennsylvania

Jörg E (2020) Greed for short selling, BoD, Norderstedt

Jurgeit L (1989) Valuation of options and financial securities subject to credit risk, DUV, Dt. Univ. Verl., Wiesbaden

Kirchner C (2007) Kampf um jeden Basispunkt, in HB, No. 76, 19.4.2007, p. 28

Kokologiannis G (2012) Risky downside speculation, in HB, 32, 14.2.2012, pp 38, 39

Kolb RW (1991) Understanding futures markets, 3rd edn. Kolb Publishing Company, Miami, FL

Kumar A (2015) Short selling, finding uncommon short ideas. Columbia University Press, New York

Landgraf R (1991) German market has accepted securities lending, in HB, No. 40, 26.2.1991, p 41

Landgraf R (2003) Securities lending comes into fashion, in HB, No. 231, 1.12.2003, p 19

Ledwig K (2017) Wertpapierleihen von Versicherungsunternehmen. Fred Wagner (ed) Verlag Versicherungswirtschaft, Karlsruhe

Leez M (2007) Wertpapierleihe - Rechts- und Verfassungsfragen der Unternehmens-steuerreform 2008. GRIN Verlag, Norderstedt

Limmert M (1994) Die Wertpapierleihe, Veröffentlichungen des Lehrstuhls für Allgemeine Bank- und Versicher- Betriebswirtschaftslehre an der Friedrich-Alexander-Universität Erlangen - Nürnberg, Herausgeber Professor Dr. Oswald Hahn, Nürnberg

McCrary S (2012) Financing techniques for short sellers. In: Gregoriou GN (ed) Handbook of short selling. Elsevier, Oxford, pp 120–122

Miller KA (1997) The US dollar repo market. In: Fabozzi FJ (ed) Securities lending and repurchase agreements. New Hope, Pennsylvania

Nazzaro AA (1997) Evaluating lending options. In: Fabozzi FJ (ed) Securities lending and repurchase agreements. New Hope, Pennsylvania

Nazzaro AA (2005) Evaluating lending options. In: Fabozzi FJ, Mann SV (eds) Securities finance, securities lending and repurchase agreements. Wiley, Hoboken, NJ

O.V. (1995) Glossary: common terms used in the repo market, in RISK REPO supplement, November 1995, pp 27–28

O.V (2004) Global securities financing, clearstream. Deutsche Börse Group, pp 1–13

O.V. (2010) Finance trader - repurchase agreements, ed. Finance Trader Internatio-nal GmbH, 2.4.2010

O.V. (2013a) Eurex, in Wikipedia, printout from the Internet, 24.9.2013

O.V. (2013b) Securities lending - unlocking the full potential of the portfolio, ed. Blackrock, printout from the Internet of 4.9.2013

O.V. (2020) Securities lending times, pp 1–27

Oechler E (1992) Securities lending and repo transactions from a banking supervisory perspective. Die Bank 10(92):567–574

Oegerli (1991) Securities Lending & Borrowing, Schweitzer Bank, 1991/3

Oho W and Hülst R (1992) Tax law aspects of securities lending and repo transactions, in DB, issue 51/52 of 18.12.1992, pp 2582–2587

Pantel S (2000) Securities lending and repo transactions. A business comparison. Term paper in the subject of Finance, Department of Economics Sankt Augustin, Bonn-Rhein-Sieg University of Applied Sciences, 27.10.2000

Parnes J (2020) Short selling for the long term. Wiley, Hoboken, NJ

Rettberg U (2009) Kampf um Kundenaufträge, in HB, No. 116, 22.6.2009, p 20

Schmidt H (1979) Liquidität von Finanztiteln als integrierendes Konzept der Bankbetriebslehre, in Zeitschrift für Betriebswirtschaft, 49th Jg., Heft 8, 1979, pp 710–722

Schmidt H (1981) Ways of determining and assessing banks' market risks, in Kredit und Kapital, 14th Jg., 1981, pp 249–286

Schmidt H (1988) Wertpapierbörsen, Munich

Sloan RS (1997) The role of carry in the equity markets. In: Fabozzi FJ (ed) Securities lending and re-purchase agreements. New Hope, Pennsylvania

Sommer U (2014) Computer trading started with a crash, in HB, 4-6.4.2014, pp 6–7

Van Horne JC (1994) Financial market rates and flows, 4th edn. Prentice-Hall Inc, Engelwood Cliffs, NJ

Printed in the USA
CPSIA information can be obtained
at www.ICGtesting.com
CBHW050513091124
PP15830800001B/11